Reading The Landscape

by

Carol McKay

First published 2022 by The Hedgehog Poetry Press

Published in the UK by
The Hedgehog Poetry Press
5, Coppack House
Churchill Avenue
Clevedon
BS21 6QW

www.hedgehogpress.co.uk

ISBN: 978-1-913499-62-4

A CIP Catalogue record for this book is available from the British Library.

Contents

CROW

Your husband has sustained a four-part proximal humerus fracture with greater tuberosity

When the fall damaged you,
you came to me, humbled,
needy and bewildered,
responding to my tentative hand.
Days passed. You bowed your head
while I cleansed you.
I kept the room dim for you.
Brought grubs and water. Fed my eyes on you.
I liked that I'd tamed you.

One day, your beak nudged the curtain.
As I entered the room, your black gloss feathers
gleamed in a panel of daylight, and I sensed
your feral heart hammering.
This time, when I reached my hand
your harsh beak hacked it. Just once.
And I knew I had to unshackle you,
unclasp the ring and chain fastened at your ankle.
Crows are not made to be captive.

I dragged the curtain aside; forced up the window. You
see-sawed low, voice raucous,
eyes black beads glistening with wisdom.
I clamped my hands behind me
as you reared your wings out, practising.
But what about me? I cried. Your claws
clacked on the countertop. Your eyes
fixed me – before you leapt for the trees;
leapt into the waiting space.

'CEILIDH'

I hear the voice of the bloodline
skirling down the hillsides,
rippling the weeds on the lochan,
skirting drumlins in the mirk,
from Treshnish via Duachy, skittering
at the watery edge of Loch Fyne,
by the illicit stills of Glasgow
to this sedate southern valley
with its rhodies and leylandii,
its kayaks in the boat pond,
its hoity toity tones
and morals. *One wee dram,*
it whispers.
Uisge Beatha! Aon deoch bheag!

In my mind, I hear my dad's
high yelping *Hyeuch!*
ghost round the corner,
my mother's rising *Well!*
to start the dancing.
Instead, I'm sitting, hands clasped
like it's Sunday.
It's all you need
to get this 'ceilidh' started,
I hear it sweet-talk.
Uisge Beatha!
One wee nip.

REFLECTION

My eyes, glassy crystals in the mirror,
measure the distances
in space and time
between red thread veins and forehead wrinkles;
assay my beach quartz teeth, lacking calcium,
while scorching water wastes
in the unplugged sink.

My hand, reaching for the glass, holds
the history of my father. So easily fractured.
The bite crunched from the whisky tumbler;
the uneven arc of his teeth
in mock-dental impression.
The morning-after's dregs amalgamated
into one glass, and downed.

My eyes, glassy crystals in the mirror,
focus refracted colours through this prism,
compose white light.

SPRING VESSEL

A response to work by Canadian ceramicist Andrea Piller

For three days in a lifeboat on that hostile grey ocean
my grandfather ached for earth without water:

footprints pressed in the white sands at Barra;
Ontario flatlands beyond the St Lawrence.

Cupped in waves, his clay heart brimming,
he dreamed of migrants, merchants, homecoming.

Flux, glost and glimmer: a full moon glazing
the cold hulls of vessels all North Atlantic drifting.

GULL FLIGHT, SUNLIGHT

A black bee bumbles on the window pane
as gulls cross morning sky, heading south west.

The starling seeks its nest in last year's roof
while buzzard settles on his ancient post.

Fox crouches for his rendezvous with shrew.
The magpie's bone horn beak tugs more stout twigs.

Lured by the spring sun's angle-shifting light,
the baby in my arms uncurls his fist.

RISK ASSESSMENT

We'd forgotten how it feels
to be drenched to the bones
like the day we drove to Moffat.

We'd set off under blue skies
that turned black as we topped out
in the honey-coloured moors
of the southern uplands.

It was dry when we arrived, so we risked it
and walked along the river under oak trees
that have withstood rain for decades,
our ears tuned to thrush song
and the Annan's warble.

Returning through the main street,
unencumbered by umbrellas,
we were defenceless when the rain
came down in torrents.

You know your hair is thinning
when those wet barbs chill your old scalp.
I was desperate for a brolly.
Rain dripped from my nose and glasses
and I cursed our lack of planning.

Water drummed on the car roof
as we stared out through misted windows.
Then the news came on the radio
about another wave of Covid.

Complacent, we'd forgotten
we are all in thrall to nature.
And some downpours defy
any risk assessment.

RINGING THE BULL

Swallows skim over farm acres
throbbing in the long days' heat –
barley crops for malting, gold
beneath the heaviest blue.

At the field edge, in the leafy shade
of alder, birch and oak
the young bull stands.

I almost see your great-grandfather
shoulder and prod the steaming beast,
and master it. Sweat coats them both.

See him run his calloused hand
down the animal's twitching flank
appraising muscle, vigour, strength.

Decisive, quick, he punches iron
clean through its fragile nasal flesh,
clamping the metal to form
a leading ring.

Who knew that you, in turn,
fresh muscled, toned, smooth-motioned,
rambling through the city streets
without a ring
could be so easily led?

BEACH

If I could bring it all back home
it would take:
two red lungfuls of ozone air;
eight fragile folds between sandy toes;
two delicate shell-likes echoing
with the roar of waves in whorls;
a onesie of skin still tingling;
a heart finely balancing in yellow light.
All this and more, to hold
scallops of alabaster.
Bleached oak antlers.
Seagull calls. All this.
Pearls of blue glass,
sand winnowing. All this
and more.

AFTER THE POETRY READING

After the poetry reading, arm in arm,
we prattled along Sauchiehall Street
about who'd made the best impression:
the one too shy for eye contact;
the boss of an American accent...

Ahead, Glasgow's towers
gleamed platinum; air burned
with the scent of wood-fired pizza;
music buffered
through a dark, open doorway.

...the poet whose words whisper-painted
fields fizzing with bumblebees and yarrow...

You drove over the high arching Kingston Bridge
through a sky late May, later
than nine in the evening blue
and we fell silent.

Below, the Clyde, garrulous with rainfall
that had gurgled down hills red-kite-feathered,
gushed between tenement embankments,
declaiming its way out to sea.

CAUSEWAY

The moon has withdrawn
all but the scattered dapples
of salt sea water
from the sandbanks
that line this causeway.

On either side
ripple pools are brimming
cups of sky.

Stranded filter feeders,
bivalves tightly fastened,
limpets clinging to water-polished stones,
are in limbo in this liminal air, sea, sand.

Where does this causeway lead?
Where has it come from?

All life's on hold, dreaming
of the fulgent, rushing tide
new moon and circumstance
will usher in.

ACCESSORIES

'Scotland records highest level of drug deaths in Europe'
The Guardian, 3 July 2018

There's a magpie complaining in the bushes
and a lone crow commandeers a sky
not even airbuses can tarnish
on this blue, blue, aquamarine
inverted-swimming-pool sky day.

I'm up early, up before the neighbours.
Up before anyone has even begun
to contemplate accessories.
Waiting for a bus into the city.

A tap on the app hints at the groaning uphill
of my double decker. Two minutes.

The magpie's throat is still rattling. A skinny cat –
striped mini-beast, barely adolescent – high tails it
out from the rosa rugosa and I remember
our old cat's tortured love affair with magpies,
scornful under her breath as they berated her
all the way home out of the willow.

How many cat-lives ago was that?
How many magpies?

Another tap on the app. One minute.

It's like any addiction: you can't live with them.
You can't live without them.

And then I wonder where you are this morning.
Have you even noticed it's morning? Have you
clean clothes to wear? Do you have something to eat
with your coffee? My bus arrives.
What are you going to choose as accessories?

PERSPECTIVE

Under this sea cliff at Davaar
the beach is an erratic tumble
of sharp-edged boulders.

Marooned on these jagged rocks,
I'm petrified –
an old woman calculating
how my brittle bones
might fare if I fall.

Between the stones at my feet
what used to be cockles
are flat, cloudy discs
worn smooth by the tides.

Suspended in the shimmer
of June sun on water, I tell myself
London is grounded on skeleton remains.

Those white cliffs of Dover,
compacted from shells,
stand, sturdy,

while Ailsa Craig the curling stone
is just a smudge on the horizon.

SYNAESTHESIA

There are people in my house
I can't see,
cross-legged on my yellow couch;
creaking the second top stair.

Ciphers, like the vowel not used
which is the key;
the organ note that sounds
though never played.

I hear the space
between the lines of what they say;
see light bend
in the pressed waves of their hair.

Some days when the cat leaps
to invisible laps
I hack my fingers through
the coded air

and google a sensory Rosetta stone
I hope to find, one day,
glancing up to catch
more than a memory of smiles.

KINTYRE

In Kintyre, geology
looks civilised.
Tablecloth corners
drape its flat, ridged hills.

Walls of water shatter
as the tide presses.
Car air vents usher in
the tang of the sea.

Swallows are the commonest bird,
fast jets over low land,
flicking and yawing
all along this green road.

WALKING THE LOWTHERS

White mist sifts
dry ice from the valley.

Sunlight transforms
black night into blue.

I pick a path with sticks,
climb from horizontal,

a tick on a living hill
whose pelt glows ochre.

Buzzard peeps overhead
break the bright stillness.

My eyes seek the sound,
ascend to the summit,

to a carousel of birds,
soft brown, cavorting,

their shadows skiing down slopes
not white, yet, with snow.

LEAF LITTER

Not a ripple disturbs the pond
in the hospital grounds.
Yellow, it reflects
the withering trees.
Like a fresh skin it's unwrinkled
even this close to endings,
untrammelled by each repeating day's
harsh human news.

Jaundiced by autumn
you and I slip hands,
witness the release
of another umber leaf.
Weightless, it falls
like a burden through the air
to drift on the pond's
smooth surface.

ENCLOSURE, PENRUDDOCK

Drystone dykes encase field shapes
the way a child wraps arms round sweets on a table:
this is my land: this mud, this root, this schist.

Green lichen stars –
like crystals grown in water glass,
like 3D paper cut-out flakes of snow,
like living coral – garland old hawthorn bones.

The top soil's rich but rock lies
just below the surface.
A coarse stone bridge leads only back in time.

FIRST FLOOR BEDROOM, PENRUDDOCK.

Gauzy scraps of chiffon flitter
beyond the glass like giddy birds.

Out of the south, blue air unfastens
blackbird trills from yellow beaks
and children's words from ruddy lips

(while jerseys, red as babies' cheeks,
race pell-mell through the playing field).

It delivers them through the window frame
with the building site drill and rookery caws
and the orange-feathered cockerel's call.

Wind gusts harry in the chimney.
Over the laptop, fingers flurry.

READING THE LANDSCAPE

I try to read encryptions in the landscape:
cold marsh-land stippled by the stiffened grass;
raggedy bracken folding into earth;
scars cut by Iron Age ploughs or
by this season's never-ending rain.

Damp cattle, mottled, matted,
graze, dreadlocked, across these tilting fields.
A white-crested river drains
down towards the sea through blackened hills.

Day is curbed. A distant fireball smoulders
while over stubble fields a flock of birds –
starlings maybe, or the fieldfares come –
squabble for rank across a smoky sky.

TIDAL GREY-OUT

The cows are black against the broad firth
against October clouds and twilit river
as we look out through the windows of this bus
aquaplaning down towards Kincardine,
towards the blade where sea cuts land,
towards evening.

Water melds with sky in aluminium.
A dull fusion
that's foreground, background:
backcloth to entire space.
Tidal grey-out replicates the sky
as water falls into water.

Across the Forth, Ineos fires and smokes –
thrawn hardman lagging from industrial days.
On the closer shore, Longannet's idle stack
blinks in brisk warning through the air.

Inside this bus's watery light,
one man laughs, pours his long tale
into another's ears. A third
has closed his eyes, head back against the rest.
He's dreaming,
not of views, but of the days he's had
and those to come.

In retrospect we might recall those silhouettes.
A glimpse of other lives.
Or let the water wash them from our minds.

ACKNOWLEDGEMENTS

Several of the poems in this collection first appeared in anthologies and literary magazines. My thanks go to their publishers.

'Ceilidh' (*Dreich* 5, 2020)
Reflection (*From Glasgow to Saturn*, 32, November 2013)
Spring Vessel (*Gutter* 15, Autumn 2016)
Beach (*Island and Sea*, Scottish Writers' Centre, 2020)
After the Poetry Reading (*Dreich* 5, 2020)
Accessories (*Gutter* 19, Spring 2019)
Synaesthesia (*The Istanbul Review* 4, Winter 2013)
Kintyre (*Blue Nib*, 2020)
Walking the Lowthers (*X: an anthology to celebrate the tenth anniversary of the Scottish Writers' Centre*. Red Squirrel Press, 2018)
Enclosure, Penruddock (*Dreich* 5, 2020)
First Floor Bedroom, Penruddock (*Landfall*, Federation of Writers, Scotland, 2017)

My thanks to Mark Davidson of Hedgehog Poetry Press for his ingenuity and inventiveness, and for all his help in bringing *Reading the Landscape* into the world.